Presenting the Past Teacher's Resources 1

Britain 1066–1500

Keith Worrall

Published by Collins Educational
An imprint of HarperCollins*Publishers* Limited
77–85 Fulham Palace Road
Hammersmith
London
W6 8JB

www.**Collins**Education.com
On-line support for schools and colleges

© HarperCollins*Publishers* Ltd 2001
First published 2001

ISBN-13 978-0-00-711462-7
ISBN-10 0-00-711462-1

10 9

Keith Worrall asserts his moral right to be identified as the author of this work.

Any educational institution that has purchased one copy of this publication may take unlimited duplicate copies for use exclusively within that institution. Permission does not extend to reproduction, storage in a retrieval system, or transmittal in any form or by any means, electronic, mechanical, photocopying, recording or otherwise, of duplicate copies for loaning, renting or selling to any other institution without the prior consent of the Publishers.

British Library Cataloguing in Publication Data
A catalogue record for this publication is available from the British Library.

Edited by Samantha Davey
Design by Ken Vail Graphic Design, Cambridge
Cover design by Derek Lee
Artwork by Peter Bull and Daniel Betts
Production by Kathryn Botterill
Printed and bound by Martin's The Printers, Berwick upon Tweed

FSC is a non-profit international organisation established to promote the responsible management of the world's forests. Products carrying the FSC label are independently certified to assure consumers that they come from forests that are managed to meet the social, economic and ecological needs of present and future generations.

Find out more about HarperCollins and the environment at
www.harpercollins.co.uk/green

Acknowledgements

Every effort has been made to contact the holders of copyright material but if any have been inadvertently overlooked the Publishers will be pleased to make the necessary arrangements at the first opportunity.

Photographs
The Publishers would like to thank the following for permission to reproduce photographs on these pages:

T = top, B = bottom, C = centre, L = left, R = right

By permission of the British Library, MS AVI f.66r, 58T

Cover image: By permission of the British Library, MS Roy 2 OCVII f.133

Realia
The Publishers would like to thank the following for references made to their work in *Presenting the Past Book One: 1066 – 1500*:

p. 37, Barbara Hanawalt, *Crime in East Anglia in the 14th Century*, Norfolk Record Society, 1979; pp. 88–89, Matthew Strickland, *War and Chivalry* (1996 Cambridge University Press); p. 91, Christopher Dyer, *Standards of Living in the Later Middle Ages* (1989 Cambridge University Press).

Contents

Introduction   4

Section One – Ruling a Kingdom: a deadly game

Matching Chart   7

Teacher's notes   8

Worksheets 1.1–1.17   10–26

Section Two – The power of religion

Matching Chart   27

Teacher's notes   28

Worksheets 2.1–2.17   30–46

Section Three – Medieval people: did they have a hard life?

Matching Chart   47

Teacher's notes   48

Worksheets 3.1–3.15   50–64

Introduction

The aim of the *Presenting the Past* series is to provide exciting and different approaches to teaching history at Key Stage 3, aimed at pupils of all abilities. Active learning is achieved through a range of teaching strategies, which relate to and support current national initiatives. These initiatives include the new National Strategy, the roll out of the National Literacy Strategy, and the introduction of Citizenship education as a National Curriculum subject. All of these impact upon the teaching of History at Key Stage 3 and it is the purpose of this series to support the teacher in delivering high quality teaching whilst, at the same time, taking on board the implications of these initiatives when planning schemes of work for Key Stage 3 History.

This teacher's guide identifies the links between *Presenting the Past Book One* and the History Programme of Study, QCA Schemes of Work (2000), the National Literacy Framework, QCA Scheme of Work for Citizenship (2001), ICT activities and Key Skills.

In addition to the series of photocopiable support worksheets there are recommendations for further extension activities. These suggestions will support less-able pupils and stretch more-able pupils in line with DfES recommendations for Gifted and Talented Pupils at Key Stage 3. Relevant worksheets are listed in brackets next to the teacher's notes relating to each pupil book unit, for example (w1.9). Where provided, warm-up activities are intended to act as an introduction to new concepts and skills and should be undertaken prior to looking at the particular topic in the pupil book.

Guidance given within this book is purely recommendation and advice. There is plenty of scope here to develop a range of teaching and learning styles. You may wish to develop your own activities from these suggestions and use the resources as a starting point to develop ideas to match your scheme of work and assessment needs according to the ability of your pupils.

Authors

Tony McAleavy is the former Humanities Advisor for Gloucestershire County Council, and a leading member of the team that produced the QCA Scheme of Work.

Andrew Wrenn is the Humanities Advisor for Cambridgeshire County Council and an expert on the relationship between Citizenship and History.

Keith Worrall is the General Inspector for Humanities, PSHE and Citizenship for Doncaster.

Paul Grey is the General Inspector for Humanities, PSHE and Citizenship at the London Borough of Havering.

Rosemarie Little has been a successful History teacher for 13 years, an LEA advisory teacher for History and a freelance History consultant.

Citizenship and Literacy Opportunities

Opportunities for producing evidence of Citizenship and Literacy can be found in the matrices at the beginning of each section. The abbreviations in these sections of the matrices relate to the NC Programme of Study for KS3 Citizenship and QCA's *Framework for teaching English: Years 7, 8 and 9*.

◆ Citizenship

Knowledge and understanding about becoming informed citizens. Pupils should be taught about:

    a the legal and human rights and responsibilities underpinning society, basic aspects of the criminal justice system, and how both relate to young people

    b the diversity of national, regional, religious and ethnic identities in the United Kingdom and the need for mutual respect and understanding

    c central and local government, the public services they offer and how they are financed, and the opportunities to contribute

    d the key characteristics of parliamentary and other forms of government

    e the electoral system and the importance of voting

    f the work of community-based, national and international voluntary groups

    g the importance of resolving conflict fairly

    h the significance of the media in society

    i the world as a global community, and the political, economic, environmental and social implications of this, and the role of the European Union, the Commonwealth and the United Nations.

◆ Literacy

NB: Opportunities for Vocabulary and Spelling are found throughout *Presenting the Past Book One*

Teaching Objectives Year 7
Sentence level

3 use punctuation to clarify meaning particularly at the boundaries between sentences and clauses;

8 recognise the cues to start a new paragraph and use the first sentence effectively to orientate the reader, e.g. *when there is a shift of topic, viewpoint or time;*

11 vary the structure of sentences within paragraphs to lend pace, variety and emphasis;

12 organise ideas into a coherent sequence of paragraphs, introducing, developing and concluding them appropriately;

Reading level

Pupils should be taught to:

1 know how to locate resources for a given task, and find relevant information in them, e.g. *skimming, use of index, glossary, key words, hotlinks;*

2 use appropriate reading strategies to extract particular information, e.g *highlighting, scanning;*

3 compare and contrast the ways information is presented in different forms, e.g. *web page, diagrams, prose;*

4 make brief, clearly-organised notes of key points for later use;

5 appraise the value and relevance of information found and acknowledge sources;

6 adopt active reading approaches to engage with and make sense of texts, e.g. *visualising, predicting, empathising and relating to own experience;*

7 identify the main points, processes or ideas in a text and how they are sequenced and developed by the writer;

8 infer and deduce meanings using evidence in the text, identifying where and how meanings are implied;

9 distinguish between the views of the writer and those expressed by others in the text, e.g. *the narrator, quoted experts, characters;*

10 identify how media texts are tailored to suit their audience, and recognise that audience responses vary, e.g. *popular websites;*

Writing level
Pupils should be taught to:

1 plan, draft, edit, revise, proofread and present a text with readers and purpose in mind;

2 collect, select and assemble ideas in a suitable planning format, e.g. *flow chart, list, star chart;*

3 use writing to explore and develop ideas, e.g. *journals, brainstorming techniques and mental mapping activities;*

5 structure a story with an arresting opening, a developing plot, a complication, a crisis and a satisfying resolution;

11 select and present information using detail, example, diagram and illustration as appropriate;

12 develop ideas and lines of thinking in continuous text and explain a process logically, highlighting the links between cause and effect;

14 describe an object, person or setting in a way that includes relevant details and is accurate and evocative;

15 express a personal view, adding persuasive emphasis to key points, e.g. *by reiteration, exaggeration, repetition, use of rhetorical questions;*

16 find and use different ways to validate an argument, e.g. *statistical evidence, exemplification, testimony;*

18 identify criteria for evaluating a particular situation, object or event, present findings fairly and give a personal view;

Speaking and Listening
Pupils should be taught to:

1 use talk as a tool for clarifying ideas, e.g. *by articulating problems or asking pertinent questions;*

2 recount a story, anecdote or experience, and consider how this differs from written narrative;

3 tailor the structure, vocabulary and delivery of a talk or presentation so that listeners can follow it;

7 answer questions pertinently, drawing on relevant evidence or reasons;

11 adopt a range of roles in discussion, including acting as spokesperson, and contribute in different ways such as promoting, opposing, exploring and questioning;

12 use exploratory, hypothetical and speculative talk as a way of researching ideas and expanding thinking;

13 work together logically and methodically to solve problems, make deductions, share, test and evaluate ideas;

14 acknowledge other people's views, justifying or modifying their own views in the light of what others say;

15 develop drama techniques to explore in role a variety of situations and texts or respond to stimuli;

17 extend their spoken repertoire by experimenting with language in different roles and dramatic contexts;

Matching Chart: Ruling a Kingdom (pages 5–51)

This section of *Presenting the Past Book One* relates to the QCA Scheme of Work unit 'How did medieval monarchs keep control?'

Presenting the Past Book One unit title	Opportunities for Citizenship (National Curriculum for KS3)	Opportunities for Literacy (QCA *Framework*)	Key Skills	Opportunities for ICT	Thinking Skills
Ruling a kingdom: a deadly game	1c, 1d	**TR** W1, 3	C, PS, WO		
Factfile: William the Conqueror	1g	R1, 4; **TR** SL7, 13	C, PS, WO	TR	
1066: The job interview	1d, 1e	S11, R6, W3, 15	C, WO	✓	
Was victory inevitable?	1g	R2, 3, 7, W3, 11	C, PS, WO		✓
Was William lucky and clever?	1d, 1g	S11, R4, 7, 8, W12, 15; **TR** R4, SL7, 13	C, PS, WO		✓
Hastings: battle to the death		R2, 7, 8, R4, 5, W1, 3; **TR** R4, SL7, 13	C	✓	
Interpreting the Battle of Hastings		R3, W3	C	TR	
They'll kill us if they get a chance	1a, 1b, 1c, 1d, 1g	S3, 12, R7, W1, 11, 14, 15	C, PS, WO	✓	✓
William's success		S12, R3, 4, 6, 7, 8, 9, W14, 15	C, PS, WO	✓ TR	✓
Royal murder mysteries: the death of Rufus	1a, 1d, 1g	S12, R7, W1, 3, 15	C, PS, WO		✓
Matilda's bid for power	1a	R7, 8, W15	C, PS, WO		✓
A licence to kill? The death of Becket	1a, 1b, 1d, 1g	S12, R2, 6, 9, W5, 11, 15	C, PS, WO	✓ TR	✓
Henry and Becket: a deadly quarrel	1a, 1b, 1d, 1g	S12, R2, 6, 7, 8, 9, W5, 11, 15	C, PS, WO	✓	✓
Royal justice	1a, 1c, 1d	R2, 6, 8	C, WO	TR	
The mystery of the kind-hearted jury	1a, 1c, 1g	R2, 4, 6, 8, W3, 5, 15	C, PS, WO	✓	✓
A king's army: cavalry and infantry	1a, 1g	R2, 6, 7, 8, W12	C, PS, WO		
John and the barons	1a, 1b, 1c, 1d, 1g	R4, 6	C, PS, WO		✓
Magna Carta	1a, 1c, 1d	R4, 6, 8, W3, 15	C, PS, WO	✓	✓
England and the Celtic lands	1a, 1b	S3, 8, R6, 7, W11, 15	C	✓	✓
The changing face of the royal castle	1d	S3, 8, 11, R4, 6, 8, W3, 14, 15	C, PS, WO	✓	✓
Royal murder mysteries: William Wallace	1a, 1b, 1c, 1d, 1g	R7, 8, 9, 10, W1, 2, 15; **TR** SL13	C, PS, WO	✓	✓
The problems faced by monarchs	1a, 1b, 1c, 1d, 1g	S3, 8, 12, R7, 8, W2, 12	C, PS, WO	TR	✓

Key:

Explanations for National Curriculum Citizenship and QCA *Framework for teaching English* abbreviations can be found on pages 5 and 6 of this book.

TR = *Presenting the Past Book One Teacher's Resources*

Key Skills abbreviations: C = Communication; PS = Problem Solving; WO = Working with Others

Teacher's Notes Section one – Ruling a Kingdom: a deadly game

Section one of *Presenting the Past Book One*, 'Ruling a kingdom: a deadly game', is intended to build up understanding of medieval monarchy through the study of a series of historical situations. This will include aspects such as royal justice, punishment and legal systems, power, warfare and rights. From the run-up to the Battle of Hastings to the death of William Wallace, pupils will identify the characteristics of medieval monarchy and what was needed in order to survive and be remembered as a successful king or queen.

Ruling a kingdom: a deadly game (worksheet 1.1)
- This activity is a warm-up task leading into the factfiles which follow, and can be aided by worksheet 1.1.
- Citizenship: you might discuss the rights and responsibilities of a monarch, or within a school, as an introduction to the activity.

Factfile: William the Conqueror
- There is the opportunity for a differentiated activity with varying degrees of support.
- You might take group feedback on the qualities of a king to move the discussion forward.
- Literacy: Spellings and understanding of the key words can be developed as homework activities or as part of an end-of-unit assessment.
- Extension activity: more-able pupils could choose three words and include them in sentences that describe William.

1066: The job interview (w 1.2, 1.3)
- The tasks lend themselves to role-play exercise with Key Skills in mind.
- Paired work or larger group work can be undertaken culminating in a role-play of the job interview by a panel, under your direction.
- Final decisions could be presented in written form through a panel spokesperson, or as a task in exercise books, perhaps leading to a larger class presentation highlighting different aspects of the interview.

Was victory inevitable? (w 1.4, 1.5)
- Pupils must identify what William might need in order to win the battle at Hastings.
- Worksheet 1.4 helps pupils to prioritise the problems William faced and to include explanations for the three problems.
- Worksheet 1.5 is an extension activity to address the similar question for Harold Godwinson.

Was William lucky and clever? (w 1.6, 1.7)
- Class discussion on this unit could include the 'what if..?' factor or a discussion related to luck, fortune and other important historical events.
- A DARTS-style worksheet has been provided to help with the text analysis.
- Worksheet 1.6 provides an alternative format for delivering this unit.

Hastings: battle to the death (w 1.8, 1.9)
- After reading through the text, you might extend the discussion with reference to the monarch today.
- Worksheet 1.8 provides an alternative approach for the less-able pupils, prompting pupils to undertake the role of historians.
- The discussion can be broadened to consider the strengths and weaknesses of the Bayeux tapestry as a historical source, introducing the idea of different ways to interrogate a source and the kind of questions you might ask (who, what, why, when and how?). This leads into the next unit about interpreting the battle.

Interpreting the Battle of Hastings
- The idea of an interpretation and its use to support a specific viewpoint will need to be introduced.
- Encourage pupils to identify possible reasons for the different interpretations shown. You might provide further examples as a stimulus.

They'll kill us if they get a chance
- The text provides opportunities for extended reading, analysis of text and awareness of sentence construction.
- Pupils could develop alternative answers to William's problems.
- Extension activity: a written report, enabling pupils to indulge in imaginative and extended writing through empathy. Suggested points to cover:
    1. Where did the Normans base themselves after the battle was over?
    2. How did William organise his army after the battle?
    3. How did they build their castles so quickly?
    4. What was feudalism?
    5. How did the Normans use their castles to repress the Anglo-Saxons?
- You might extend the discussion to talk about local or nearby Norman castles.
- A DARTS activity may be appropriate to investigate the text of 'The Harrying of the North'.

William's success
- Citizenship: linked through the study of political systems and the development of Parliament under a medieval monarchy.

- You may wish to divide the class and allot questions 1–4 accordingly, and provide appropriate ICT materials like the BBC History File (Medieval Britain).
- You might encourage pupils to debate William's qualities as a king from different perspectives, which could also be completed as an extended writing exercise for more-able pupils.

Royal murder mysteries (w 1.10)
- An interview and interrogation worksheet is provided to support this section, which could also be undertaken as a short role-play exercise.

Matilda's bid for power
- As part of a warm-up activity you might revisit the topic of what makes a 'good king/queen' posing the questions: Did Matilda have the right stuff? Why was she chosen? What problems did she face? Who objected to her as queen?
- A role-play could be performed, or pupils can undertake an extended writing exercise with different headings, to identify Matilda's strengths and weaknesses.

A licence to kill? The death of Becket (w 1.11, 1.12)
- A re-enactment of the murder scene and the interrogation of witnesses through a police-style investigation is an ideal teaching strategy for this unit (see worksheet 1.11).
- Worksheet 1.12 is a timeline activity to help less-able pupils to identify the short-term events leading up to the murder. More-able pupils could look at the long-term factors. A large classroom timeline could also be produced using ICT.
- Extension activity: consider the implications of this event in terms of citizenship, i.e., was it right for a king to act in such a way? What rights did Becket have? Should Henry have taken advice from others before he flew into a rage?

Royal justice
- Citizenship: you might assess the investigation of crime and punishment with original sources, by comparing the criminal justice system today with medieval times. There is plenty of scope to look at all elements of law.

The mystery of the kind-hearted jury
- This activity could be undertaken as a role-play exercise with a reconstructed trial. Pupils could identify the strengths and weaknesses of this jury system.
- There are clear links here with PSHE and Citizenship curriculums.

A king's army: cavalry and infantry (w 1.13)
- Worksheet 1.13 is recommended for less-able pupils in order to handle the amount of text in this unit.

John and the Barons (w 1.14)
- Reference could be made to earlier work on monarchs, revisiting the key issues about their success and their problems.
- Citizenship: links to the rights and responsibilities of monarchs and ordinary people in the middle ages.
- A worksheet has been provided to differentiate the tasks for less-able pupils but is appropriate for all abilities.
- Reproducing the text so that John's good and bad points can be underlined would be valuable for less-able pupils.

Magna Carta
- Citizenship: there are links with the rights and powers of people in medieval and modern times.

England and the Celtic lands (w 1.15)
- Pupils can use what they have learnt of the Magna Carta to determine how these rights were translated into practice in England, Wales, Scotland and Ireland.
- The extended writing activities address Literacy.

The Changing Face of the Royal Castle
- This unit addresses how castles evolved to meet different geographical and political needs of the time.
- Further work could be developed relating to castles in your region.

Royal murder mysteries: the death of William Wallace (w 1.16, 1.17)
- The focus here is to utilise modern film techniques in the study of history.
- Focused teacher input will be required in order to help less-able pupils.
- Worksheets 1.16 and 1.17 provide a foundation warm-up involving class discussion and brainstorming about heroes and villains, and are suitable for all levels.
- A role-play of the trial of Edward for the murder of Wallace could be implemented at the end of this topic.
- Pupils could break up the sources into sections and write a description or news report of the trial from both sides.
- Citizenship: you might discuss justice, fairness and the rights and powers of the medieval monarchy.

The problems faced by monarchs
- Pupils are encouraged to suggest a hypothesis by which problems were resolved.
- The selection and deployment of relevant information to make their choices could form part of a class-based activity or display on the issues of medieval monarchy.

Ruling a Kingdom — 1.1

What makes a successful leader?

You are going to decide what characteristics are needed to be a successful leader.

Step 1

1. Look at the people listed in the chart. For each person choose four qualities from the list on the right which they would need to be good at their job. Write the qualities you have chosen on the chart in the column marked 'Successful'.
2. Then choose four things that would prevent them from being good at their job. Write these on the chart in the column marked 'Unsuccessful'.

- Kind
- Clever
- Loyal
- Determined
- Listener
- Generous
- Educated
- Honest
- Warrior
- Sensible
- Fair
- Selfish
- Harsh
- Talker
- Cautious
- Cruel
- Greedy
- Thoughtful
- Worried

	Successful	Unsuccessful
Football Manager		
Prime Minister		
Headteacher		

Step 2

3. Could you add two more words of your own in each column?
4. Share your ideas with a partner and then compare them with two other people in your class.
5. How are your ideas similar and different to others?

	Successful	Unsuccessful
King		

Step 3

- Now do the activity again but think about a king instead.
6. What would a king need to be successful and unsuccessful?
7. Share your ideas with a partner and then compare them with another group.

You Decide

- From Step 3, decide for yourself – did William have the makings of a successful king?

Extension Activity

- What weaknesses do you think the medieval kings had?
- What other factors influenced their behaviour?
- Who usually decided if someone was a 'successful' or 'unsuccessful' king?

Ruling a Kingdom 1.2

The job interview: questions

Fill in the form below for each candidate. You should use a new form for each one.

Candidate Name:

Place/Country of Origin:

Related to Edward the Confessor: Yes ☐   No ☐

Candidate's Current Job Title:

Questions to be asked: Marks

1

Reply: ☐ /10

2

Reply: ☐ /10

3

Reply: ☐ /10

Total: ☐ /30

Ruling a Kingdom

1.3

The job interview: results

1st Place: _____

Mark ⬜/30

2nd Place: _____

Mark ⬜/30

3rd Place: _____

Mark ⬜/30

◆ We think the best person for the job is _____

because _____

_____

◆ We think the most unsuitable person for the job is _____

because _____

_____

◆ Therefore, the panel has decided to offer the post of King of England to

_____

Extension Activity

1 Write a short letter to the two unsuccessful candidates explaining to them why they didn't get the job. Make a list of three or more reasons why they were unsuccessful before you begin your letter.

Ruling a Kingdom 1.4

Prioritising the factors needed by William to win the Battle of Hastings

Step 1

1 Working in pairs, cut out and place the words from the list below onto the fish skeleton diagram. Decide which factors would be the most important if William was to win the Battle of Hastings against Harold Godwinson. Start from the head, most important factor, and work towards the tail, least important factor.

- Strength
- Leadership
- Good weather
- Weapons
- Food and supplies
- Experience
- Energy
- Determination
- Allies/friends
- Horses
- Speed
- Transport

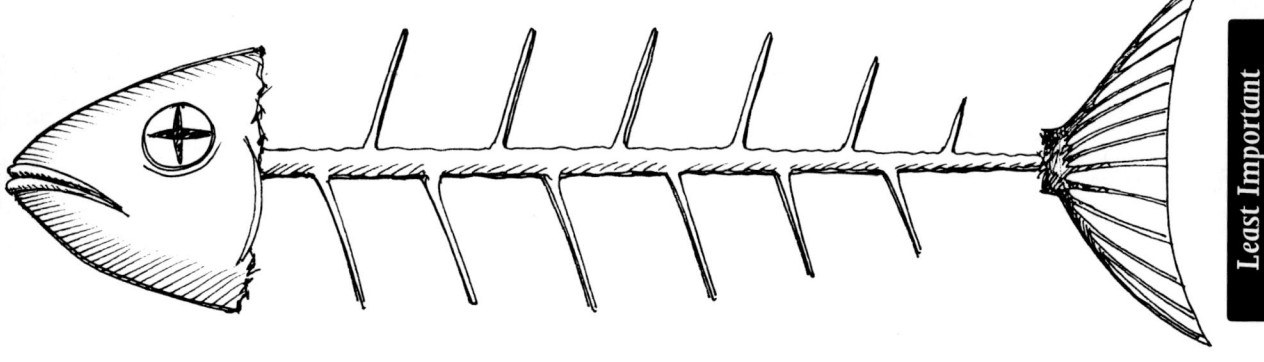

Most Important · Least Important

Ruling a Kingdom

1.5

Prioritising the factors needed by Harold to win the Battle of Hastings

Step 1

1 Can you identify the key factors for Harold Godwinson from the list below that led to his defeat at Hastings?

- Tiredness after the long march from Stamford Bridge
- Battle weary after defeating Harald Hardrada
- Deserters returning home to gather in the harvest
- Anger at reports of the Normans plundering nearby villages
- Poor preparations and too much celebration the night before the battle
- No cavalry, unlike the Normans
- Over-confident after defeating the vikings

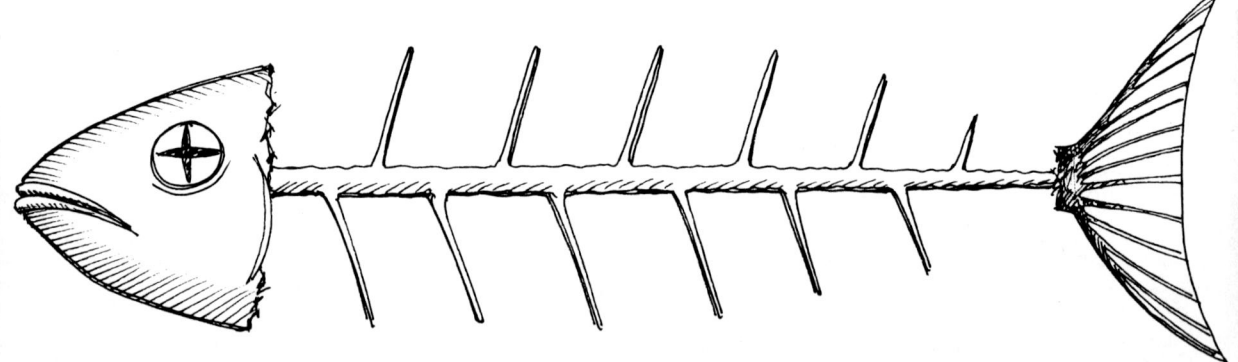

Most Important — Least Important

Step 2

2 Now that you have looked at the list, place the words on the diagram in order of importance. Start from the head, most important factor, and work towards the tail, least important factor.

3 Are there any other factors which are not included in the list?

Ruling a Kingdom — 1.6

Was William lucky and clever?

Stage 1

What Harold did	What William did
In the summer of 1066, Harold Godwinson organised a huge army and a massive fleet of 700 ships to stop William invading. In August, the soldiers and sailors said that they had to go back to their homes to help with the harvest. On 8 September Godwinson sent the soldiers and sailors home.	By July, William was ready to attack. Most people thought he would attack immediately. Instead William waited and waited. He knew that most of the English soldiers and sailors would need to go home before the summer was over to help with the harvest.

Stage 2

What Harold did next	What William did next
Just after Harold Godwinson sent his soldiers home, Hardrada and his Norwegian army landed in Yorkshire. Harold marched north to fight him. As he travelled towards York he quickly gathered a new army. After a rapid march, his army reached Stamford Bridge where the Norwegians were based. They slaughtered the Norwegian army and Hardrada was killed.	During most of September William couldn't sail across the English Channel, because the wind was blowing in the wrong direction. On 27 September, the wind changed. William and his army, the Normans, crossed safely. With Harold Godwinson busy in Yorkshire no one tried to stop his army when they landed. Meanwhile Hardrada, one of his two enemies, was killed by Harold without William having to lift a finger.

Step 1

1 Highlight or underline the reasons why Harold should wait.
2 Highlight or underline the reasons why Harold should fight.

Step 2

3 Who do you think was the most lucky and clever?

I think _____

was more lucky and clever than _____

because _____

Presenting the Past 1 Teacher's Resources © HarperCollins Publishers 2001

Ruling a Kingdom

1.7

What should Harold have done?

On your diagrams about William's victory and Harold's defeat we did not mention ... luck. Very often the outcome of important events in history have been determined by luck.

Some historians now use the question *'what if...?'*

Both William and Harold had choices and decisions to make. Should Harold have marched to meet William at Hastings? Should he have waited to see what William would do?

What would *you* have done?

Step 1

Remember, William's journey to England had already been delayed by the weather. Winter was not far away and William needed to have access to food and shelter before the winter set in. Now complete the sentences below.

◆ My advice to Harold would be _____

because _____

◆ If Harold had done this then I think he would have _____

and _____

Ruling a Kingdom

1.8

Hastings: battle to the death (1)

Step 1

1 Draw a small picture of your head. Place it over the head of one of the English foot-soldiers in the picture on page 14 of your textbook.

2 Now imagine you are that foot-soldier fighting in the Battle of Hastings. Describe what you can hear, see and smell.

Step 2

3 Using what you have learnt about the battle, highlight on the extracts below and on worksheet 1.9 any information which tells you about the points listed in box 1.

---

1 William's:
- Confidence
- Self-Belief
- Fight for his cause
- Skills as a soldier
- Skills as a leader

---

2 The start of the fighting

The English passed the night without sleep, in drinking and singing, and in the morning marched quickly to battle. The Normans passed the whole night in prayer and held a church service in the morning.

The English were all on foot, armed with battle-axes. They protected themselves by joining their shields together, and this made them into a very strong force. The Normans had foot-soldiers and cavalry (soldiers on horse-back). Their foot-soldiers stood in the front armed with bows and arrows, while their cavalry was at the back.

William of Malmesbury

---

3 What did William do during the battle?

Before the fighting started William looked confident and calm. He spoke to his troops, telling them that they would win because God was on their side.

When the fighting began, William shouted to his soldiers to encourage them. He was the first to rush forward to attack. He fought in the middle of the enemy. He seemed to be everywhere, fierce and furious. Three of his horses were killed under him. This did not frighten him. His bodyguard urged him to be careful, but he still continued to fight. No doubt the hand of God protected him, though the enemy aimed many spears at him.

William of Malmesbury

Ruling a Kingdom 1.9

Hastings: battle to the death (2)

4 Fierce fighting and clever plans

For many hours there was fierce fighting and neither side gave way. Many were killed on both sides. Then William thought of a good battle plan — he ordered his troops to pretend to run away. The solid wall of the English fell apart as they chased the fleeing Normans. The Normans turned around and attacked the English. This trick led to the death of many English but it did not end the battle. The English regrouped on the hillside and killed the Normans as they struggled up the hill.

William of Malmesbury

5 What did Harold do during the battle?

The battle went on for hours, with first one side and then the other doing better. The English were ready to carry on fighting as long as Harold lived. He was very brave. Not content to be a general, he fought like an ordinary soldier. He killed many of the enemy at close quarters. Sometimes he killed a soldier and horse with a single blow. The Normans were afraid to approach him.

William of Malmesbury

6 How did the battle end?

The battle continued as long as Harold was alive. He was able to stop the English from giving up. The Normans were not able to kill him in hand-to-hand fighting. It was only a long-range arrow that brought him down. The arrow pierced his brain and Harold was killed. One of the Norman soldiers hacked at his legs as he lay on the ground. The English soldiers then gave up fighting and ran. The Normans chased after them until night fell. William and the Norman soldiers had won.

William of Malmesbury

Extension Activity

4 Using the same extracts highlight the reasons why you think Harold lost the battle.

You are now doing what historians do when they investigate the past. They **analyse** (study) historical sources which describe or tell us about an important event in the past. But you can also use the same sources in different ways. For example, as you have done, to find out about William's actions in the battle and also Harold's mistakes before and during the battle.

Ruling a Kingdom

1.10

The death of William Rufus: interview and interrogation

You are going to interview Henry about the murder of his brother, William Rufus. What questions would you like to ask? You have read the story of William Rufus, now you have the opportunity to find out what really happened.

Step 1
1 What questions would you ask?

I/We would ask

-
-
-
-
-

Step 2
2 Do Henry's answers provide you with any evidence for the questions below?

- Did Henry have a motive?
- Who would benefit most from William Rufus's death?
- What happened to Henry after William Rufus's death?

Step 3
3 Now write your account of the incident. What other evidence might help you to solve this mystery?

- I/We would need _____

- This would tell me/us _____

- So, I/we think that William Rufus was _____

  we think this because _____

Ruling a Kingdom 1.11

The death of Becket

Step 1

1 On the timeline below, fill in the dates and events from when Henry became king to the death of Thomas Becket.

1154 — Henry II, son of Matilda, becomes king of England

December 29 1170 — Four of King Henry's knights quarrel with and kill Thomas Becket in Canterbury Cathedral

Ruling a Kingdom

1.12

Investigation into the murder of: Thomas Becket

Investigating Officer:

Witness statement given on (date):

Witness name:

Occupation:

Location at time of incident:

What did you see?:

Questions to ask the witness:

1

2

3

Witness reply to question:

1

2

3

Supporting evidence:

Further action as result of interview:

Ruling a Kingdom   1.13

The siege of Rochester

Heavy casualties

In 1215, towards the end of the reign of King John, there was a war between John and some of his barons. The barons seized the royal castle at Rochester. John was very angry and besieged them. The castle was very strong and the siege lasted two months. John and his knights could do little to get the barons out of the castle. Skilled cross-bow men inside the castle shot at anyone they saw outside. Many of John's army were killed in this way.

Let's eat the horses!

The barons and their army inside the castle could not go outside without being killed by John's army. They began to run out of food and supplies and began to starve to death. The knights from the barons' army inside the castle could make no use of their expensive war-horses so they killed them and ate them.

Cut off their hands and feet!

John got frustrated that the barons refused to surrender. He ordered some daring foot-soldiers from his infantry to go to the castle walls. Under a deadly rain of cross-bow fire from the castle, they made fires at the bottom of the walls and hacked away at the stone. Eventually the walls began to collapse. The barons still refused to surrender. They ordered their injured men to leave the castle to save food for those who remained. As these men came outside they were captured by John's army and punished by having their hands and feet cut off.

Hang all the cross-bow men!

Finally, the rest of the barons and their army were forced to surrender. John wanted to kill them all. He later changed his mind and let them live, with one exception: he ordered that all the cross-bow men should be hanged because they had already killed so many of his own men.

Step 1

1 Highlight or underline evidence which tells you:
- Horses were not very important during the siege.
- Foot-soldiers played an important role in the siege.
- Food was in short supply during the siege.
- Skilled cross-bow men were important during the siege.

Ruling a Kingdom

1.14

King John: successful king or unsuccessful king?

Step 1

1 From the text on page 40 and page 41 of your textbook, identify three good points and three bad points about King John. Write them in the columns below.

Good	Bad
◆	◆
◆	◆
◆	◆

Step 2

2 Now that you have looked at the evidence, you have to decide if King John was a good king or a bad king.

◆ I think John was a _____ king.

◆ I think this because _____

_____

_____.

Presenting the Past 1 Teacher's Resources © HarperCollins Publishers 2001

Ruling a Kingdom

1.15

England and the Celtic lands

> **Step 1**
> 1 Look at the information on pages 44 and 45 of your textbook and use this to fill in the spaces to answer the question below.
> 2 Do you think that, overall, the English kings were successful in their attempt to control the other people of the British Isles?

The English kings tried to conquer Ireland by _____.

Their actions were _____

because _____.

The English kings tried to conquer Scotland by _____.

Their actions were _____

because _____.

The English kings tried to conquer Wales by _____.

Their actions were _____

because _____.

Overall I think the English kings were _____

because _____

_____.

Other factors to be considered might be _____

_____.

These factors were also important because _____

_____.

Ruling a Kingdom

1.16

Hollywood hero or vile villain? (1)

Before we look at William Wallace we need to be clear what we mean by hero and villain.

Step 1

1 Choose your three favourite heroes and three villains from any film or television programme you have seen. Write these in the columns below.

Hero	Villain
◆	◆
◆	◆
◆	◆

Step 2

2 Write one sentence on a hero you have chosen and explain why you have chosen them, or what it is that makes them a hero.

3 Write one sentence on a villain you have chosen and explain why you have chosen them, or what it is that makes them a villain.

Often people are liked or disliked in history for what they have done, but your view may be influenced by which 'side' you are on. To ordinary people Robin Hood was a hero because he took money from the rich and gave it to the poor. But, to King John and the barons Robin Hood was a thief because he took money away from them.

Step 3

So, what about William Wallace?

4 Fill in the two charts on the next page using the information you have learnt about Wallace. In the first chart choose three things that King Edward would have thought were good about William Wallace, and three things he would have thought were bad. In the other chart, choose three things that ordinary Scottish people would have thought were good about Wallace and three things they would have thought were bad.

Presenting the Past 1 Teacher's Resources © HarperCollins *Publishers* 2001

Ruling a Kingdom

1.17

Hollywood hero or vile villain? (2)

King Edward's thoughts about Wallace

Good	Bad
◆	◆
◆	◆
◆	◆

Scottish people's thoughts about Wallace

Good	Bad
◆	◆
◆	◆
◆	◆

Step 4

5 *Using the charts you have filled in, complete the following sentences.*

◆ Overall, I think Edward would have felt that William Wallace was _____

because _____
_____.

◆ Overall, I think Scottish people would have felt that William Wallace was _____

because _____
_____.

Matching Chart: The power of religion (pages 52–78)

This section of *Presenting the Past Book One* relates to the QCA Scheme of Work unit 'How did the medieval church affect people's lives?'

Presenting the Past Book One unit title	Opportunities for Citizenship (National Curriculum for KS3)	Opportunities for Literacy (QCA *Framework*)	Key Skills	Opportunities for ICT	Thinking Skills
The power of religion		R4	C, PS,	TR	
The heretic test: will you be burnt alive?	1a, 1b, 1g	SL11, 12, 17	C, PS, WO		
The Church is everywhere	1a, 1f	S8, R2, 6, 7, W2, 3	C, PS, WO	TR	✓
Welcome to Hell	1a, 1b, 1h	R3, 6, 8, 9, W3, 15	C, PS, WO	TR	✓
How to get to Heaven	1a, 1b	R4, 6, W1, 2, 3; **TR** SL13	C, PS, WO		
Monks and nuns	1b, 1f	R6, 7, 8	C, PS, WO		✓
Which order should I join?	1b, 1f	S12, W2, 15	C, PS, WO		✓
Religion and the law	1a, 1f, 1g	R6, 7, W3, 5, 11, 15	C, PS	✓ TR	✓
Let's go on pilgrimage	1b	S8, R2, W2, 14, 16	C, PS	✓	✓
Holy journey or holiday: were all pilgrims religious?		R4, 5, 6, 8, W2	C, PS, WO		
The perils of pilgrimage		S12, R7, W3, 11, 15	C, PS, WO		✓
Chaucer and the Church	1a	S3, 8, 11, R6, 8, 9, W11	C, PS, WO	TR	✓
Why were the Jews mistreated?	1a, 1b, 1c	R6, 7, 8, W3, 15	C, PS, WO	TR	✓
Was the Church doing its job well?	1a, 1b, 1c, 1f	S8, 11, 12, R7, 8, W3; **TR** SL3, 7, 13	C, PS, WO	✓	✓
Why was the Church so important?	1b	S3, 8, 11, 12, R1, W1, 11, 12	C, PS, WO	✓	✓

Key:

Explanations for National Curriculum Citizenship and QCA *Framework for teaching English* abbreviations can be found on pages 5 and 6 of this book.

TR = *Presenting the Past Book One Teacher's Resources*

Key Skills abbreviations: C = Communication; PS = Problem Solving; WO = Working with Others

Teacher's Notes Section two – The power of religion

The focus of this section is to address religion and the extent of the power of the Church in the middle ages. The activities are intended to develop pupil understanding of how and why the Church was so powerful. The role of the Church in all aspects of society and medieval life is reinforced throughout this unit. This includes the medieval Church as an instrument of social control, the importance of the concept of heaven and hell, the political role of Church leaders and the role of the church within the legal system of the middle ages.

The power of religion (worksheet 2.1)

- As a warm-up you might have supplementary material available, such as images of the medieval church, to give pupils prior visual stimulus.
- Suggested headings for notes have been provided on worksheet 2.1 to enable pupils to build a picture of the medieval Church.

The heretic test: will you be burnt alive? (w 2.2)

- There is the opportunity to undertake a role-play covering the mock trial of a heretic. Preparation would be necessary concerning the format of the trial and the make-up of the court.
- Worksheet 2.2 supports this activity using a trial format appropriate for a role-play or a written class activity.

The Church is everywhere (w 2.3, 2.4)

- The activity supports literacy strategies which pupils may encounter in a different context e.g. in an English lesson.
- Worksheet 2.3 provides a differentiated version of the activity in this unit, prompting pupils to begin comparing the medieval and modern Church.
- You might wish to compare the role and power of the medieval Church with the Church in Britain today. How do the roles differ? What evidence do we have of the Church being actively involved in society today?
- Pupils will need to be made aware of the extent to which the medieval Church was a major landowner when assessing its power.
- Further support for this activity could be a diagrammatic representation of the power of the Church, such as a venn diagram (medieval and modern Church on either side). Pupils could choose similarities and differences from a list of keywords, placing them on the diagram where applicable.
- Pupils could develop research skills in class or as a homework activity to be completed over several lessons. More-able pupils could undertake further research, to develop a more complex overview of the relevance of the Church to society today.

Welcome to Hell

- There is plenty of supplementary material to bring this section to life, e.g., the BBC History File series has extracts from sermons about hell and pictures of medieval church wall paintings.
- Images of medieval representations of hell would be an excellent stimulus here.
- Pupils might produce their own sermons or illustrations of hell according to the medieval Church.
- Literacy: pupils could read and analyse the text structure and content. Less-able pupils might undertake this through a DARTS-style activity.

How to get to Heaven (w 2.5)

- Using worksheet 2.5 pupils can produce their own steps to heaven from a medieval perspective and consolidate learning in an extended writing format.
- This could be expanded through class discussion. Who, in the eyes of the Church, deserved to go to heaven? What must someone do to get to heaven?
- Citizenship: there is the opportunity to make links with issues concerning the social and moral values of a society and Religious Education.

Monks and Nuns (w 2.6, 2.7)

- Worksheets 2.6 and 2.7 provide a card-sorting activity to enable pupils to establish the hardships and benefits of life as a medieval monk or nun.

Which order should I join? (w 2.8, 2.9)

- The matching task here could be undertaken as a paired or group activity with various grouping strategies coming into play e.g. gender, mixed ability, peer relationships.
- Key Skills: problem solving, working with others and communication are evident here, as well as oracy through listening to the views and ideas of others.
- A worksheet has been provided to support this activity but sound prior preparation is essential.

The story of Odo (w 2.10, 2.11)

- These two worksheets are extra to the pupil book and provide an exciting opportunity to consider stereotypes in history.
- Odo is a Church leader with clear political aspirations and an example of the varied roles medieval Church leaders had, which is very different from Church leaders today.
- Literacy strategies are used for tasks 1 and 2. Task three highlights the question of Church leader or politician? This links in with whether bishops were always holy men and reinforces the concept of the bishop as warrior, politician and Church man.

- There is plenty of scope to extend the study and address the issue further as a class or small group discussion.

Religion and the law
- Citizenship: this unit focuses on the criminal justice system in relation to the Church.
- You might explore the concept of sanctuary further with reference to asylum seekers and political refugees if it is appropriate to the group.
- The activity is an opportunity for role-play as it takes pupils into the medieval mind by looking at the various methods of trial. It could also be extended as a homework activity.
- An extended writing exercise might be developed here. Pupils could describe each of the trials and prioritise them using an agreed set of criteria, e.g., fairness, justice, equality and punishment.

Let's go on pilgrimage
- This topic can be linked to R.E., English and Citizenship.
- A short piece of imaginative writing describing their own pilgrimage to a special place provides a good pupil warm-up activity prior to starting the main tasks.
- You could also bring in elements of English with extracts from Chaucer's *Canterbury Tales*.

Holy journey or holiday: were all pilgrims religious? (w 2.12, 2.13)
- A worksheet has been provided to identify the needs of pilgrims and the perils they might have encountered on their journey. This activity could be set as a homework task or an extension piece for more-able pupils.
- Worksheet 2.13 differentiates the task using a DARTS-style activity to access the concepts covered.

The perils of pilgrimage (w 2.14)
- A DARTS worksheet has been provided to differentiate the text and tasks in this unit.
- You might develop cross-curricular links through this unit working with, for example, the R.E. unit on Islam and the Haaj.

Chaucer and the Church (w 2.15)
- There is an opportunity here for a more in-depth study of Chaucer.
- Less-able pupils may need a more structured framework for the activities provided on worksheet 2.15.
- Extension activity: You might extend the worksheet by asking pupils to argue that some people were doing a good job and others a bad job, using *however, for example,* and *because* to link sentences. They could also give an opinion of what they thought Chaucer's view was using *overall*.

Why were the Jews mistreated? (w 2.16)
- You may wish to undertake the task here as a narrative with a focus on oracy.
- For less-able pupils tasks 1 and 2 could be completed as DARTS activities.
- You might refer to the BBC History File Medieval Realms which refers to the massacre of the Jews at York.
- A worksheet has been provided which addresses literacy strategies in this section of work. This could be undertaken as an extension, as homework or as a class activity providing pupils with the opportunity to feedback their findings to the rest of the group.

Was the Church doing its job well? (w 2.17)
- Worksheet 2.17 has been provided to differentiate task 4 and encourage pupils to develop higher order thinking when interpreting historical sources.
- You might also give pupils a hypothesis to test using the evidence provided, and begin a discussion about expected findings, comparing results in a plenary at the end of the section.

Why was the Church so important?
- The activity here draws together prior learning using prompts to develop knowledge and understanding of religion in Britain today.
- For less-able pupils a writing frame may be appropriate using three bullet points. Further support materials might also be necessary in order to support less-able and extend more-able pupils.

The power of religion

2.1

The power of the Church

> **Step 1**
> As you work through this section make some notes under the headings listed below. You can use them later as a writing frame to help you explain why and how the church was so powerful in the middle-ages.

- Church and government

- Church and knowledge

- Church and charity

- Church and land

- Church and punishment (hell)

- Church and rewards (heaven)

- What must I do?

The power of religion 2.2

The trial of a heretic!

Name of accused: _____

Charged with crime of: _____

The judge is (teacher name): _____

> **Court Officer:** 'Discussion of the charge between the Judge and the Jury will now begin. The accused may be allowed to contribute and argue his/her view by answering the questions of the Jury.'

1 Would it be a good idea to have the Bible in English as well as in the old language, Latin?:

   Answer: _____

2 Abbeys, where monks and nuns live, have got lots of land and are very rich. Should we close them down and give the money to the poor?:

   Answer: _____

3 Some churches have the bones of dead, holy people on display. Is this a good idea?:

   Answer: _____

> **Court Officer:** 'The jury will now retire to consider the accused's answers.' …
>
> … 'The jury have come to a decision – it is time for the verdict.'

The jury believes that the correct answers to its questions should be:

_____

We therefore find the accused (name):

_____

Guilty/not guilty of the charge:

_____

He/she should be: released immediately | Yes | No |

                    OR

                    burnt to death as a heretic | Yes | No |

Presenting the Past 1 Teacher's Resources © HarperCollins *Publishers* 2001

The power of religion

2.3

How can the Church help you?

Look at the problems the medieval people in the box below have. They would like the Church to help them with their problems. You are going to think about how the Church can help.

> Thomas: 'I am interested in science. How can I find a job that will let me find out about the world?'
>
> Eleanor: 'I'm desperate. I've got no money, no job and two babies to feed.'
>
> George: 'I can read but I can't afford to buy any books. Is there a library around here?'
>
> Henry: 'I want some land so that I can be a farmer and can feed my family.'
>
> James: 'I'd like my children to go to school.'
>
> Anne: 'My old mother is very ill. She needs to be looked after in a hospital.'
>
> Adam: 'I'd like to work as a civil servant.'

Step 1

1 Choose four people from the box on the left, think about their problem and answer the three questions. This will tell them how you think the Church can help.

Name: _____
How can the church help you?
_____
_____

What should you do?
_____
_____

Who would you ask for help for each of these problems today?
_____
_____

Name: _____
How can the church help you?
_____
_____

What should you do?
_____
_____

Who would you ask for help for each of these problems today?
_____
_____

Name: _____
How can the church help you?
_____
_____

What should you do?
_____
_____

Who would you ask for help for each of these problems today?
_____
_____

Name: _____
How can the church help you?
_____
_____

What should you do?
_____
_____

Who would you ask for help for each of these problems today?
_____
_____

The power of religion

2.4

Medieval and modern Churches

Step 1

Now you have looked at how the Church can help people, you can find out more by completing the following tasks:

1 Do some research on the internet or in your library about the role of the Church today in the areas listed below.

2 For each one think about how the Church contributes to the development of each area.

- Charity
- Peoples' spiritual needs
- Education
- Shelter and housing projects

Step 2

3 Are there any other key areas not included in this list which you have discovered?

I think the Church still has an important role in society today because

_____
_____
_____
_____
_____
_____
_____
_____
_____
_____
_____
_____

Presenting the Past 1 Teacher's Resources © HarperCollins *Publishers* 2001

The power of religion 2.5

How to get to heaven

Step 1

1 Use the form below to create your own guide to the medieval Church. Start by looking back at the pictures of hell on page 57 of your textbook. In the same style as these pictures, draw your own picture of what your personal idea of hell would be in the box provided below.

A beginners guide to the medieval Church by (name):

_____

[drawing box]

My view of hell

If you want to get to heaven then follow these steps:

1) DON'T:	2) DO:
◆ _____	◆ _____
◆ _____	◆ _____
◆ _____	◆ _____
◆ _____	◆ _____
◆ _____	Three points of your own:
◆ _____	◆ _____
◆ _____	◆ _____
	◆ _____

If you follow these 2 steps then you will get to heaven.

OR

You could join a religious order ... but which one?

The power of religion

2.6

Should you become a monk or nun? (1)

Monks and nuns were not allowed to get married.

Monks did interesting work as writers, doctors and book illustrators.

Kings, queens and other famous people were friends with monks and nuns. These celebrities often stayed at monasteries.

Ordinary monks and nuns spent a long time in church. There were at least eight services that they had to attend every day.

There was a chance of promotion to a powerful job. If you became abbot or abbess (the most important monk or nun in the monastery) you could be one of the most powerful people in the country.

The abbot or abbess had total power. A monk or nun who disobeyed could be beaten or locked up and put in chains.

Step 1

1 Working with a partner, cut out the cards on worksheets 2.6 and 2.7 and read the explanation on each card. Sort the cards into two piles:
- ◆ Good points about becoming a monk or a nun.
- ◆ Bad points about becoming a monk or a nun.

The power of religion 2.7

Should you become a monk or nun? (2)

Bedtime was about seven o'clock and monks and nuns got up at two o'clock in the morning.

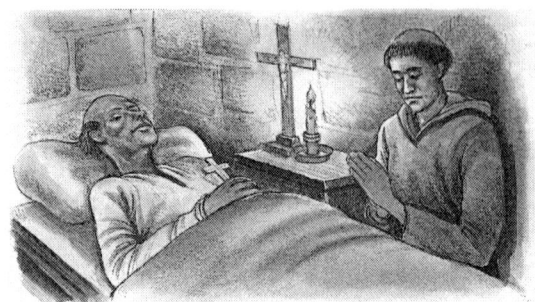

People thought that monks and nuns had a better chance than anyone else of going to heaven.

There was only one meal a day during summer and meat was forbidden except during illness.

Nuns did skilful artistic work as embroiderers.

Monks (but not nuns) were given a first class education.

Private property was not allowed. Monks and nuns were supposed to share everything.

Step 2

2. From your 'good' pile identify the three most important reasons you might have for becoming a nun or a monk.
3. From your 'bad' pile identify the three least important reasons why you might want to become a nun or a monk.
4. Share your ideas with another group. Think about how your ideas are similar or different?

The power of religion

2.8

Which order shall I join? (1)

Thomas 'Most religious orders are too soft. I want a really strict order so I can be sure of getting into Heaven when I die. The world is a wicked place and I want to get far away from ordinary people so I can concentrate on God.'

James 'I don't even know if they'll have me in a monastery. I come from a poor family and I can't read or write. I like doing practical things like farming and building work. I'd like to help better educated monks in their holy work.'

Henry 'I'm torn between wanting a life of prayer as a monk and wanting to help people in trouble. I'm very religious but I'm also interested in medicine and looking after the sick. Is there an order that will help me to keep up my interest in both these things?'

Matthew 'I don't want to be locked away in a monastery. I want to be out in the world talking to ordinary people about Jesus. I don't want to join a really rich order because followers of Jesus should have no money.'

Joan 'I want to devote myself completely to God's work. I like the ideas of St Francis who says we must give up everything to be like Jesus. Of course, as a woman, I cannot copy Francis and wander from place to place. But I can hide myself away and spend my life in prayer.'

Matilda 'I want to serve God but I'm not a religious fanatic. I like prayers but I don't want to be in church all day and all night. I like nice food and good company. To be honest, I'm a bit of a snob and I only feel at home with other ladies like me from the top families of the land.'

Step 1

1. Look at the job adverts on worksheet 2.9. Working in pairs match up the needs of the 6 people with the most appropriate religious order for each of them. Then, give each religious order a mark out of 10 depending on how strict it was.
2. Which was the most strict? Which was the least strict?

Step 2

3. Cut out the cards and place them on your desk in order of strictness.
4. Does your order match up with those of other groups?
5. Why do you think some religious orders were more strict than others?

The power of religion

Which order shall I join? (2)

Benedictine Nuns
Upper class ladies only need apply.

As the oldest and wealthiest order of nuns, we are quite choosy about new members. We particularly welcome new nuns from royal and noble families. Life here is not too strict. You will spend some of your time in church but you can also spend time talking to friends and doing hobbies like embroidery.

Cistercian Lay Brothers
Are you poor, badly educated, unemployed but keen on religion?

We have the right place for you. Even poor men are welcome as Cistercian Lay Brothers. You do not need to be able to read but you will have to work very hard helping the Cistercian monks around the monastery and on their farms. You will serve the monks and will help them to carry out their holy work.

Cistercian Monks
Want to get away from it all?

We offer a strict life in monasteries set in wild remote countryside. You will hardly ever see other people and this will help you to concentrate on your life as a monk. This is the life for the monk who is really serious about getting to Heaven.

Augustinian Canons
You want to be a monk but you also want to get out and help people.
The Augustinians could be the answer to your prayers. Our members are known as canons because they're different from ordinary monks. They spend a lot of time in church but they also help local people and run a number of hospitals.

Poor Clares Nuns
You don't have to be called Clare to join us but if you join you will be very poor!

We are named after Saint Clare, the sister of Saint Francis. Like her brother she wanted to copy Jesus by living a simple life and giving away all her money. As a Poor Clare you will never leave your monastery and will spend nearly all your time praying.

Franciscan Friars
*Want to see the world
AND
get to Heaven?*

Life as a friar could be right for you. With us you will have an interesting and varied life. You will go from place to place preaching to people. Our order was founded by the Italian, Saint Francis. He believed that we should give all we have to the poor.

The power of religion

2.10

Were bishops always holy men? The story of Odo (1)

The Church was run by bishops. Every city with a cathedral had a bishop who was in charge. Not all of these men were very holy. Let's meet Bishop Odo who was the half-brother of William the Conqueror. He was a very important bishop. We know a lot about Odo from other people's writing. If he had told his story we can imagine he would have said something like this:

'My brother's been dead a long time and soon I will be joining him. I am Odo. You've never heard of me? Typical. I suppose you know all about my older brother William, Conqueror of the English. I should call him my half-brother really. We had the same mother but different fathers. William had all the luck. When he was only 8 years-old he became Duke of Normandy. His education was very simple: he was just taught how to fight. For me it was much more boring. As a younger brother, I was brought up to become a Church leader. I spent long hours learning to read and write in Latin when I wanted to be out playing and fighting. When I was thirteen I was made Bishop of Bayeux.'

'Now that I'm close to death I must be honest about my sins, otherwise I'll surely burn in Hell for all time. I've broken lots of the rules of the Church. When I was young I had girlfriends, although I wasn't supposed to. There was one who was special to me and we had a son, even though we weren't married.

'I have loved money, power, beautiful things. The Church says these things are wrong but I cannot deny my sins. The Church also forbids priests like me from fighting but I fought alongside my brother at the Battle of Hastings. If you ever get a chance, look at the tapestry in the cathedral at Bayeux. It shows me in the thick of the fighting, helping to win the battle for the Normans.

'Afterwards William rewarded me well. He gave me more land than any other person. Overnight I became amazingly rich. My new land was all over England but my great stronghold was in Kent. Whenever William had to leave England to go back to Normandy, I ruled the country for him.'

'It's strange. I was suddenly one of the richest men, but I wanted more and more. I told my men to take as much as they could from the English. I even stole from the Church. Some of my army got carried away and went round robbing English churches. If anyone objected to our activities we beat them up and burned

Bishops were supposed to be peaceful but Odo fought in the Battle of Hastings alongside his brother, William the Conqueror.

The power of religion

2.11

Were bishops always holy men? The story of Odo (2)

their houses to teach them a lesson. The English hated me. I shipped the money back to Normandy where it paid for a magnificent new cathedral at Bayeux. After fifteen years of power I lost everything. All my wealth and power depended on William. We had a terrible argument. He thought I was plotting against him and I was thrown into prison. He sentenced me to life imprisonment and took all my land and money.

'That was a terrible time. I was kept for six years in chains in a dungeon. William would not forgive me. The Pope, as Head of the Church, wrote and said that it was wrong to lock up a bishop. William ignored this and refused to release me. If William hadn't died I would still be rotting in prison.

'After his death I regained my freedom. I suppose I should have behaved myself once I was free but I rebelled against the new king, William Rufus. My army burnt and looted those villages in Kent that belonged to the king. We took everything we could steal to Rochester Castle. William Rufus was furious. He besieged the castle. I almost starved to death. It was so bad that I decided to surrender. Rufus said that he was going to hang me but later he calmed down. I was ordered to leave England for ever.

'So I returned to Bayeux in France.'

'After a few quiet years I became restless again. Many people wanted to fight against the Muslim people who ruled Jerusalem. I decided to join them. I thought, "If only I can reach the holy city of Jerusalem surely God will forgive all my sins". But it seems that it is not to be. I am old and I have fallen very sick. I've reached Sicily but there is still far to go. It seems that I will die here, far from Jerusalem.'

Odo giving advice

Bishop Odo died in Sicily in 1097.

Step 1

1 How would you describe Odo? Choose three of the following **adjectives** (describing words) to fit his personality:

◆ Kind ◆ Fierce ◆ Holy ◆ Energetic ◆ Greedy ◆ Humble ◆ Hypocritical ◆ Repentant

2 For each adjective find some facts in the story that support your choice.

3 The job of a bishop was to be a good Church leader. Was Odo good at his job? Explain your answer.

The power of religion

2.12

A guide to pilgrimage?

Step 1

1 Using the words in the box at the bottom of the page and what you have learnt so far, fill in the blanks in the sentences to make your own Pilgrim's Guidebook.

Pilgrim Guidebook

- On a medieval pilgrimage I would need to take:

  _____, _____,

  _____ and _____.

- But as I go on my pilgrimage I would have to be careful because I might meet _____.

- Other dangers I might face could include

  _____, _____,

  _____, _____.

- I would take a _____ with me to protect me.

- Once I arrived at Canterbury I would visit the _____ of _____.

- After my _____ to Canterbury I would return home safe in the knowledge that God will be pleased with me.

- food
- supplies
- robbers
- money
- wild animals
- bad weather
- storms
- floods
- clothes
- pilgrimage
- relic
- shrine
- St Thomas Becket
- Canterbury

Presenting the Past 1 Teacher's Resources © HarperCollins Publishers 2001

The power of religion

2.13

Were all pilgrims religious?

Source 1: from *The Book of Margery Kempe*, written in 1463, by Margery herself.

'When I finally reached Jerusalem I thanked God for letting me see this marvellous place. I was so happy to be in the holy city that I fainted. Two Dutch pilgrims saved me from falling off my donkey. It was evening and we went straight to the Temple church and stayed there all night and most of the next day. Then we toured the city with monks who showed us all the places where Jesus had been. When I heard about the sufferings of Jesus I wept and sobbed. When we reached Calvary where Jesus died I was so upset I could not stand up.'

Source 2: from an anonymous story called *The Tale of Sir Beryn*, written in about 1400.

Some pilgrims arrived at Canterbury and first of all went to an inn. One pilgrim went straight to the taproom where the beer and wine was served. The barmaid cried 'You are welcome, brother.' She said this with a very friendly look, as if she wanted a kiss. He wasted no time but grabbed her by the middle and gave her a kiss as if he had known her for years. They started talking and she told him that she was sad because her boyfriend had died recently. He tried to cheer her up. He said his name was Jenken. She replied that she was called Kit. Jenken looked Kit straight in the face in a loving way. He sighed and began to sing a song called 'Now, love, do me right'.

Step 1
1 Highlight or underline in each source the points listed below:
- Why each person went on a pilgrimage.
- What they did on a pilgrimage.
- Who wrote the source and when.

Step 2
2 Can you trust the sources?
3 Are there any sources you would not trust?
4 Why might you not trust all of the sources?

The power of religion

2.14

The perils of pilgrimage

Where to stay:

Do a deal with the owner of a galley in Venice. Make sure that you get a place on the top deck for in the lowest it is right smouldering hot and stinking. To get a good place and be looked after you will need to pay 40 gold coins for your boat trip and back again to Venice. Buy a feather bed, a mattress, two pillows, two pair of sheets, and a quilt.

What to take:

Take with you three 10 gallon barrels, two full of wine and one with water. Keep these for emergencies as the ship's captain should give you wine and water and feed you twice a day. Take another barrel with you to use as a toilet for your room in the galley. When you call into ports beware of the fruit, for if you are not used to them they can lead to diarrhoea. If an Englishman gets that sickness, it is a marvel not to die of it.

What to eat:

Take a large wooden chest for your things. Put a lock and key on your chest. Sailors and other pilgrims will try to steal from you. In your chest keep supplies of bread, cheese, spices, and other food. For though the captain will give you food, sometimes it will be stale bread, sour wine, and stinking water. Then you will want to go away and eat on your own. Take a little pot and frying-pan and other dishes for your own cooking. Buy a bird-cage and half a dozen hens, and buy millet seed to feed them.

Once you get there:

Stay in the Holy Land thirteen or fourteen days. Look after your knives and other small things that you carry with you, for the Saracens are friendly but they will steal from you what you have if they can. When you ride out from Jerusalem to the River Jordan, take with you bread, wine, water, hard cheese, and boiled eggs, enough for two days, for there is none for sale on the way.

Avoid illness:

And if you go out to the desert where our Lord Jesus Christ fasted forty days and forty nights, it is very hot. When you come back, make sure you drink no water, but rest a little, and then eat bread and drink clean wine without water. In that great heat, water starts a great diarrhoea or fever, or both; then you can easily die.

Step 1

1. Highlight or underline all the things that the author thinks pilgrims should take on their journey.
2. Highlight or underline all the things that could go wrong on the way to Jerusalem.
3. Highlight or underline all of the things that tell you getting to Jerusalem was difficult.

The power of religion

2.15

Chaucer and the Church

> **Step 1**
> 1 Fill in the form below for each of Chaucer's three pilgrims. You should fill in a new form for each character.

Pilgrim name (invent one): _____ **Occupation:** _____

Lifestyle of pilgrim:

- ◆ _____
- ◆ _____
- ◆ _____
- ◆ _____

Rules for people working for the Church: Tick the boxes which best describe
or match the lifestyle above

- ◆ Live in a very strict and simple way. ☐
- ◆ Wear cheap plain clothes and do not try to look good. ☐
- ◆ Eat very little meat. ☐
- ◆ Spend your time on holy activities: praying, preaching and looking after other people. ☐
- ◆ Have very few things of your own and give any spare money or food to the poor. ☐

> **Step 2**
> 2 Now complete the sentences below using the information on your three profiles.
>
> - ◆ The person I looked at was _____ .
> - ◆ From the evidence I have studied I think that _____
>   did/did not follow the rules of the Church. I think this because
>   _____ .
> - ◆ However, _____ .

The power of religion

2.16

Why were the Jews mistreated?

The story of the Jews of York

A leading Jew called Benedict died, in York, in March 1190. A gang of local people broke into the dead man's house. They killed his widowed wife and his children and stole all his money. The gang attacked other Jewish families, beating and robbing them. As a result, all the Jews in York fled to the royal castle. In the past, the king had protected them. However, the king was out of the country and there was no one who would help them.

The Jews barricaded themselves in the castle. They were surrounded by an armed Christian mob led by Richard Malebisse. Like many of the leaders of the mob, Malebisse had money problems and he owed a lot of money to some of the Jews. The mob burned all the records of money owed to the Jews so that they didn't have to pay it back.

The Jews knew that they could not stay in the castle forever. They were sure that the mob were going to murder them in a brutal way. The Jewish rabbi (a leader of the Jewish Church) made a grim decision. He told all the Jews that to escape being captured by the Christians they must commit suicide. Each man killed his own wife and children. The rabbi then killed the men and set fire to the castle, before killing himself.

Step 1

1. Read the passage about the treatment of the Jews in York in 1190.
2. Now highlight or underline any words which tell you why the Jews of York were treated so badly.
3. Highlight or underline any words which tell you why the Jews were terrified of their Christian neighbours.

Step 2

4. Look at the picture of the Jews in York Castle on page 74 of your textbook. If you had been there, what would you see, hear and smell?
5. Think about what you would have done if you had been a Jew in York at this time.
6. What would you have done if you had been a Christian in York in 1190?

The power of religion

2.17

Was the Church doing its job well?

Step 1

◆ People sometimes disagree about the past because they select different information when they are deciding what life was like.

1 Explain how you could reach different views of what the Church was like in medieval times depending on what information you choose, by completing the paragraphs below.

a If I wanted to show the Church in a bad light I would select information such as:

◆ _____

◆ _____

◆ _____

I would choose these 3 types of evidence because they show in different ways what was wrong with the Church, for example _____
_____
_____.

b If I wanted to show the Church in a good light I would select information such as:

◆ _____

◆ _____

◆ _____

I would choose these 3 types of evidence because they show in different ways that the Church was doing well, for example _____
_____
_____.

c By selecting certain types of evidence I can _____
_____

However, I could show both viewpoints by _____
_____

or by _____

Matching Chart: Medieval people (pages 79–110)

This section of *Presenting the Past Book One* relates to the QCA Scheme of Work unit 'How hard was life for medieval people in town and country?'

Presenting the Past Book One unit title	Opportunities for Citizenship (National Curriculum for KS3)	Opportunities for Literacy (QCA *Framework*)	Key Skills	Opportunities for ICT	Thinking Skills
Medieval people: did they have a hard life?	1a, 1c, 1f, 1g	R6, 8	C, PS, WO		✓
Show me the money: the Domesday Book	1a, 1c, 1d	S12, R1, 9, W1, 3, 12, 14	C, PS, WO	✓	
Finding out more about medieval people		R3, 4, 6, 8, W3	C, PS, WO	TR	✓
Meet the villeins	1a, 1c, 1d, 1e	R5, 6, 8, W3	C, PS, WO		✓
The power of the lord	1a, 1c	S3, 8, 11, R7	C, PS	TR	✓
Did chivalry make life better?	1a	S12, R4, 8, W3, 15	C, PS	TR	✓
Did charity make life better for the poor?	1a, 1c, 1f	R8, W3, 15	C, PS		✓
Fairytale or nightmare: running away to a town	1a, f	R6, 8, SL1, 12, 13	C, PS, WO	TR	✓
Was living in London a pleasure or a pain?	1a	R4, W2, 11, 16	C, PS	✓ TR	✓
How smelly were medieval towns?	1c	R4, W2, 11, 16	C, PS	TR	✓
The strange science of medieval medicine		R3, 6, 8, W3, 14	C, WO		✓
The curse of the Black Death	1a	R6, 8, W3, 14, 15	C, PS	TR	✓
After the Black Death: was everybody happy?	1a	R5, 6, W3, 14, 15	C, PS, WO		✓
The Peasants' Revolt	1a, 1c, 1d, 1g	R2, 6, 8, W3, 14, 18	C, PS, WO	✓	✓
Death at the Tower of London	1a, 1c, 1d, 1g	S12, W14, 15	C, PS	✓	✓
How hard was life?	1a	R4, W1, 2, 5, 11, 12, 18	C, WO	✓	✓

Key:

Explanations for National Curriculum Citizenship and QCA *Framework for teaching English* abbreviations can be found on pages 5 and 6 of this book.

TR = *Presenting the Past Book One Teacher's Resources*

Key Skills abbreviations: C = Communication; PS = Problem Solving; WO = Working with Others

Teacher's Notes Section three – Medieval people

This section develops pupil awareness of: the different lifestyles of people in the middle ages, how the wealthy supported their lifestyle by taking from the poor, what primary and secondary sources tell us about medieval life, the structure of medieval society, the contribution made by the Church to the lifestyle of the poor, disease and health. Citizenship is a key underlying theme throughout, addressing a range of rights, powers and social and moral values relevant to medieval society and worthy of comparison with modern society. By reinforcing pupil knowledge and understanding of medieval government and society pupils have the opportunity to extend their awareness of how different aspects of medieval life impacted upon the various levels of society.

Medieval people: did they have a hard life?
- Citizenship: clear links with democracy and power
- The text is quite lengthy and you might wish to space it onto separate sheets to make it more accessible for less-able pupils.

Show me the money: The Domesday book (worksheet 3.1)
- A worksheet has been provided to develop this activity and lead into the work on the Domesday survey.

Finding out more about medieval people (w 3.2)
- You may wish to make the text here more accessible for less-able pupils. To support this a worksheet has been provided which includes a table and headings.
- Literacy: might be developed through use of text, specialised vocabulary and meanings of key words – dictionary work could also be an appropriate activity.
- You might extend the discussion prompted in tasks 1–4 to include diet, food, housing, and family, making a comparison with pupils' present day experiences.

Meet the villeins (w 3.3)
- A worksheet has been provided to help define the similarities and differences between the middle ages and modern times.
- You may wish to differentiate the worksheet to support the less-able and extend the more-able.

The power of the lord (w 3.4)
- Worksheet 3.4 aids the selection and deployment of relevant information in this activity, through an extended writing task.
- Pupils might undertake a short role-play to illustrate their findings.
- The activities here enable a variety of teaching strategies to be utilised as a means of developing pupils' knowledge and understanding.
- Citizenship: you might develop a study of accepted social and moral values in the middle ages.

Did chivalry make life better? (w 3.5)
- Worksheet 3.5 is intended to help pupils summarise the behaviour of medieval knights.
- Extension activity: more-able pupils could undertake a more complex statement and analysis of the significance of chivalry in relation to medieval society.

Did charity make life better for the poor? (w 3.6)
- Worksheet 3.6 supports task 2 using a writing frame to enable pupils to structure their ideas and put them into an appropriate form. This could also be extended for more-able pupils.

Fairytale or nightmare: running away to a town (w 3.7)
- Worksheet 3.7 accompanies the task, and could also aid a class presentation. All pupils can use the writing frame to make a judgement using the evidence.
- There is the opportunity for some imaginative writing here. This could be set as a homework or an extension task.
- The activity may need supplementing with additional source materials either from other secondary texts, library resources or ICT materials downloaded from the Internet.

Was living in london a pleasure or a pain? (w 3.8)
- Worksheet 3.8 is a thinking-skills frame to help pupils develop their knowledge and understanding of life in a medieval city. This could be used individually by pupils or as part of a collaborative learning exercise.
- Task 2 might be amended to consider the following questions: what does the evidence tell us? Were people really better off in a medieval town than in the countryside? What other problems might people have faced living in a medieval town?
- Extension activity: undertaking individual research on one particular aspect of medieval town life.

How smelly were medieval towns?
- A warm-up activity could involve pupils brainstorming about their own home and what hygiene facilities they have.
- There is scope to address a whole range of sources about medieval health, hygiene, disease and medicine and you may wish to relate some narrative about the horrible conditions in medieval towns.

- Extension activity: more-able pupils might develop this activity by investigating the reasons for the differences between health and hygiene based upon class and social status.

The strange science of medieval medicine (w 3.9, 3.10)

- A warm-up worksheet leads into this activity helping to stimulate thinking.
- Literacy: you might develop pupil knowledge by providing a list of key words which pupils will need to be able to spell and understand, perhaps use dictionaries as an integral part of the activity (see worksheet 3.10).

The curse of the Black Death (w 3.11, 3.12)

- There are clear links to be made here with the AIDs epidemic, leprosy in under-developed countries and elements of global citizenship/Geography.
- Extension activity: pupils might research the Black Death in a wider European context i.e., where did it come from? How did it spread? What factors encouraged its spread? Why was it so devastating in Europe and Britain?
- Worksheet 3.11 provides DARTs exercises and a short written summary to aid investigation, linking in with task 4.
- ICT: There are several good quality CD-ROMs available to support the learning activities in this section.
- You might complete this section with a short role-play or hot-seat exercise about the impact of the Black Death, choosing different characters from a medieval village to present the different views people had about the causes of the Black Death.
- Worksheet 3.11 would support you in the planning and delivery of this activity.
- Worksheet 3.12 will enable pupils to differentiate between the 'winners' and 'losers' in different parts of medieval society following the Black Death.

After the Black Death: was everybody happy? (w 3.13)

- There is the opportunity for a short role-play exercise with worksheet 3.13 provided to give you a framework.
- Alternatively, using the same structure, the exercise could be undertaken as an extended writing homework or extension task.
- Task 1 is quite high level and demanding of all pupils. Less-able pupils can still make a judgement by completing the task as one sentence answers on the significance of the Black Death.

The Peasants' Revolt (w 3.14)

- The key question in this section is: why might some people have been unhappy about the changes brought about by the Black Death?
- You may wish to summarise the key points from the previous unit on the important changes at all levels of medieval society as a result of the Black Death.
- A warm-up brainstorming session could identify the long and short term causes using the following questions: what grievances did people have? Who was peoples' anger directed at the most? Why were these people singled-out? What types of people joined the Peasants' Revolt?
- Citizenship: you might refer to Citizenship throughout when talking about rights and responsibilities, justice fairness and democracy.
- A DARTS-style worksheet has been provided on an account of the mob attack.
- More-able pupils might wish to identify more complex themes and dimensions e.g., social and class conflict.
- A short role-play would enable pupils to differentiate the causes and reinforce the concept of class conflict and socio-economic factors. This could be undertaken in pairs or small groups as an extension exercise if required.
- Extension activity: more-able pupils could extend their understanding by using a more complex range of sources.

Death at the Tower of London

- Citizenship remains a key aspect of this section.
- Some key questions appropriate for a warm-up activity might be: how are they similar as people? How are they different? Why might this be?
- You might ask pupils to produce a more detailed character profile, highlighting personal factors and giving a clearer view of their individual significance within a wider historical context.
- Pupils might produce task 1 as a letter to a family friend or fellow rebel describing their role in the Peasants' Revolt and reasons why they joined it.

How hard was life? (w 3.15)

- There is an opportunity for role-play in question 4. Pupils might wish to perform their role-play for the rest of the group giving their interpretation of the narrative. Worksheet 3.15 will support the less-able pupil through the activity.
- Extension activity: more-able pupils could draw together the broader themes and concepts making a balanced judgement about a whole range of issues addressed in this section and throughout the whole book.

Medieval People

3.1

Domesday profile

Step 1

1 Complete the report below for each of the five pieces of Domesday evidence on page 81 of your textbook, using the evidence and your imagination.

A Domesday Report by: _____

Name:
Status/Title:
Occupation:
Wealth/Income:

Name:
Status/Title:
Occupation:
Wealth/Income:

Name:
Status/Title:
Occupation:
Wealth/Income:

Name:
Status/Title:
Occupation:
Wealth/Income:

Name:
Status/Title:
Occupation:
Wealth/Income:

Medieval People

3.2

Finding out more about medieval people

My Key Words

Punishment	Famine	Disease	Farming	Diet

Step 1
1 For each of the headings above write 3 key words into the boxes. Use the evidence on pages 82 and 83 of your textbook to help you.

Step 2
2 Now write a sentence on each heading. Include in your sentence the three key words you have written in the spaces above. If you are unsure of the meaning of any of the words you have chosen look them up in a dictionary and write out a definition.

Medieval People 3.3

Meet the villeins

Step 1

1 Now that you have met Hugh and Alice, see how many differences and similarities you can find between how they lived and how you live now. Fill in the boxes below with all the similarities and differences you can think of, along with examples from your life.

Differences

The villeins	The way I live today

Similarities

The villeins	The way I live today

Medieval People 3.4

The power of the lord

Step 1

1 Using the information you have gathered so far about life in the middle ages from the Domesday Book, archaeological evidence and the villeins — Hugh and Alice — imagine you are a villein and write a letter to the local lord, complaining about the everyday hardships you are having to face.

- You could include some or all of the points listed below.
- You may wish to include some other factors not on this list.

◆ Diet	◆ Famine	◆ Housing
◆ Farming	◆ Punishment	◆ Working without pay
◆ Disease	◆ Taxes	◆ An absent landlord

Step 2

2 As well as complaints, think about and include in your letter some of the changes you would like to see which would make life better for you and your family.

Address: _____
_____
_____

Date: _____

Dear Lord _____,
I am writing to complain about _____
_____
_____
_____
_____
_____
_____
_____

Medieval People

3.5

Did chivalry make life better?

Step 1

1 What evidence is there that knights obeyed or broke the rules of chivalry? Fill in the boxes below, using what you have learnt to help you decide whether knights were good or bad.

Knights were good because they:	Knights were bad because they:
◆	◆
◆	◆
◆	◆
◆	◆
◆	◆
◆	◆
◆	◆

Step 2

2 Now look at the points you have written in the chart and complete the following sentences.

Overall, I think knights were _____

_____

_____.

I think this because _____

_____

_____.

Medieval People   3.6

Did charity make life better for the poor?

- The rich were always kind to the poor.
- The rich were sometimes kind and sometimes mean to the poor.
- The rich were never kind to the poor.

You Decide

- Choose one of the sentences above which you think describes what actually happened in medieval times. Write your answer below.

I think the rich were _____

_____.

I think this because _____

_____.

- For each of the other two statements give a reason why you think they **do not** describe what actually happened.

- _____
  _____
  _____

- _____
  _____
  _____

Medieval People   3.7

Running away to a town

Step 1

1. Imagine you are a villein and you are thinking about running away to the town. If you decide to go, what problems would you face? What could you look forward to?
2. Record these in the boxes below.

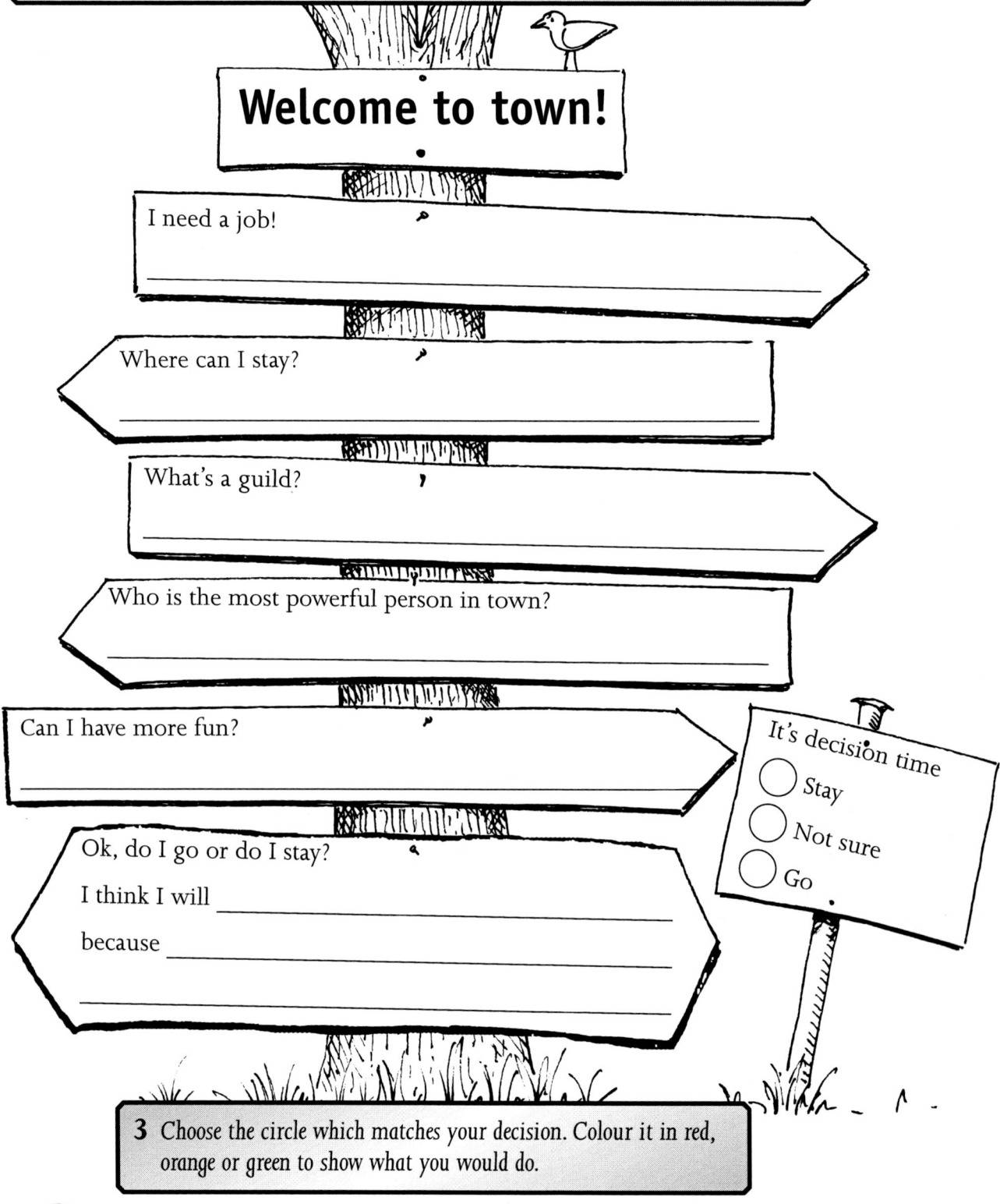

Welcome to town!

I need a job!
_____

Where can I stay?
_____

What's a guild?
_____

Who is the most powerful person in town?
_____

Can I have more fun?
_____

Ok, do I go or do I stay?

I think I will _____

because _____
_____

It's decision time
○ Stay
○ Not sure
○ Go

3. Choose the circle which matches your decision. Colour it in red, orange or green to show what you would do.

56   Presenting the Past 1 Teacher's Resources © HarperCollins Publishers 2001

Medieval People 3.8

Was living in London a pleasure or a pain?

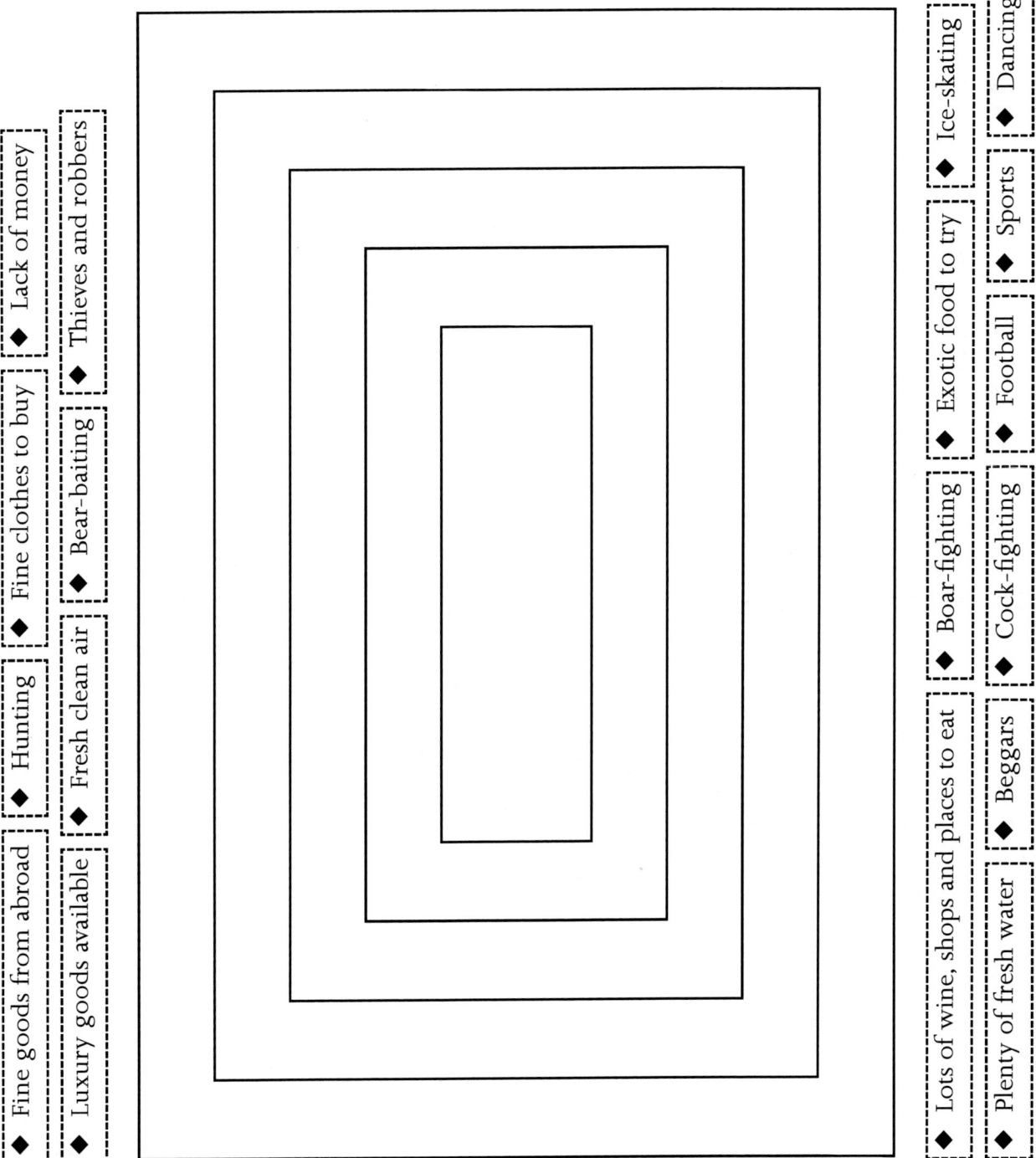

- Lack of money
- Thieves and robbers
- Fine clothes to buy
- Bear-baiting
- Hunting
- Fresh clean air
- Fine goods from abroad
- Luxury goods available
- Ice-skating
- Dancing
- Sports
- Exotic food to try
- Football
- Boar-fighting
- Cock-fighting
- Lots of wine, shops and places to eat
- Beggars
- Plenty of fresh water

Step 1

1. Cut out the cards above which show good and bad things about living in London.
2. On the diagram above place your 'good' cards nearer to the centre and 'bad' cards further away.
3. In which part of the diagram do you have the most cards?
4. Overall, would you have wanted to live in London in the middle ages?

Medieval People 3.9

The strange science of medieval medicine

Step 1

1 Write a caption for the picture explaining to the public what this picture is about.

_____

_____

Step 2

2 Imagine you are present in this picture. Write your name above one of the people.

3 What can you see, hear and smell? What are you discussing? What questions are you asking?

4 What happens next?

Medieval People   3.10

Vomiting and bleeding

Key Words
- Urine
- Humours
- Yellow bile
- Black bile
- Phlegm
- Blood
- Diagnose
- Treatment
- Physician
- Excess
- Vomit

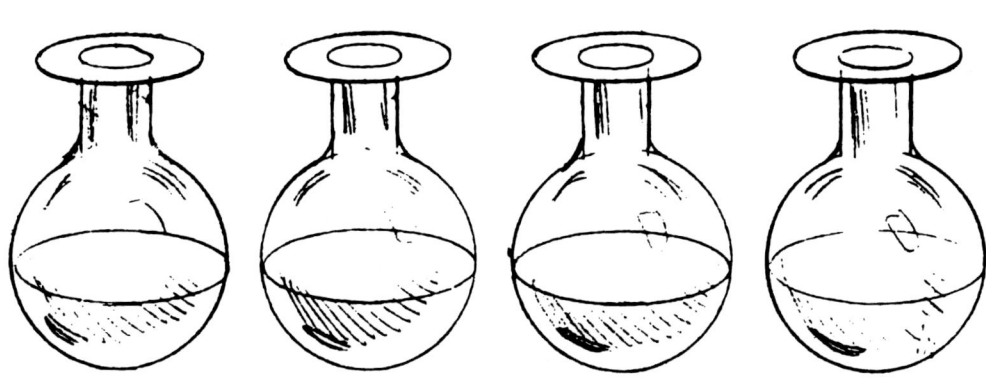

Step 1
1 Write a paragraph about why these words were important in medieval medicine. You may wish to write a different sentence for each word.

These words were important in medieval medicine because _____

Medieval People

3.11

The curse of the Black Death

> **Step 1**
> 1 Highlight in the text the things people did to avoid catching the Black Death.

'Those who lived became very frightened. Most made a selfish decision: they tried to get away from the sick to save themselves.'

'Some shut themselves up in houses where no one had been sick. They tried to eat healthy food. They refused to speak to anyone who had been near the sick.'

'Others spent their time getting drunk and having wild parties. They went from tavern to tavern, drinking huge amounts of wine. Sometimes they entered other strangers' houses and helped themselves to anything inside.'

'People ignored sick members of their own families. People were so terrified that brothers and sisters refused to help other members of the family. Husbands and wives left each other to die and mothers and fathers abandoned their children. Only a few servants stayed with the sick for very high wages.'

> **Step 2**
> 2 Now imagine you are a poor villein living in the countryside. Write a paragraph describing what you would do if your family caught the disease. Use the writing frame below to help you.
>
> In order to avoid catching the Black Death I would do four things:
>
> ◆ _____
>
> ◆ _____
>
> ◆ _____
>
> ◆ _____
>
> But, even if I did all of these things _____

Medieval People

3.12

The survivors of the Black Death

> **Step 1**
> 1 It's now two years since the plague died out. You and a friend are discussing the Black Death. Talk between yourselves about the effect the Black Death has had on your lives.
> ◆ One character should talk about the positive aspects of the Black Death. The other character should talk about the negative aspects of the Black Death
> 2 You should end your role play in agreement by deciding – was the Black Death all bad?
> Include in your role play the key points listed below:

Before the Black Death	Changes after the Black Death
◆ The countryside was overcrowded with people. The rents paid to lords were very high. Many people had tiny farms or no land at all. If the harvest was very bad they starved to death.	◆ There were fewer people and there was plenty of land to share. Rents paid to lords went down and the size of farms increased. With more land farmers grew more food for themselves and there was less risk of starvation.
◆ There were many people who were desperate for work. They would do jobs for very low wages just to get some money.	◆ There was a shortage of workers. Lords had to pay more if they wanted workers, otherwise the workers would go to work for a different boss. So, wages went up and workers had more money to spend.
◆ Women found it particularly hard to get work. Lords and other bosses were men and they gave the best jobs to men. Women were paid less even when they did the same job as a man.	◆ There were more opportunities for women who wanted to do paid work. Lords needed workers badly and they realised that they needed to make more use of women workers. Some women were now able to get the same pay as men.

Presenting the Past 1 Teacher's Resources © HarperCollins Publishers 2001

Medieval People

3.13

Was everybody happy?

Step 1

1 Using what you have learned about the Black Death, fill in the table below. For each group of people tick whether the Black Death was good or bad for them and write down what changes it brought to their lives.

Impact of the Black Death

	Good	Bad	Changes
Peasants			
Lords			
Priests			
Women			

Step 2 Good or bad?

2 Count up the number of ticks under 'good' and the number of ticks under 'bad'.

3 Write the word (good or bad) which has more ticks in the left-hand bowl of the scales and the word with fewer ticks in the right-hand bowl.

Step 3

4 For some the Black Death was _____

because _____,

however, for other it was _____

because _____.

The winners were _____.

The losers were _____.

Overall, I think the Black Death was _____

because _____

_____

Medieval People

3.14

The Peasants' Revolt

'The mob stormed everywhere, destroying the houses and property of any rich men and lawyers. They beheaded Lord John Cavendish, one of the king's leading judges. They placed his head in the market place of Bury St Edmunds. They also captured their landlord, the prior of the abbey of Bury St Edmunds and cruelly put him to death. His headless body was stripped and left in an open field for five days because no one dared to carry him away for fear of the fury of the country people. The mob entered the town of Bury, carrying the prior's head on a lance. To make fun of the prior and John Cavendish, they held together the two heads on the tops of lances as if they were kissing each other.'

1 _____

2 _____

3 _____

4 _____

Step 1
1 Highlight or underline four types of people in the text who were attacked by the mob.
2 Place them on the list at the top of the page
3 Why do you think these people in particular were attacked?

Lord John Cavendish, Chief Justice of England
Lord John Cavendish was one of the country's chief judges. There was a great shortage of workers because of the Black Death. Those who were left demanded higher wages. A law was brought in saying that no one should have a pay rise. Judges, like Lord John Cavendish, went round the country to check that this law was being obeyed. Workers who asked for a pay rise were fined or imprisoned by the judges.

Prior John Cambridge, Bury St Edmunds Abbey
The prior was in charge of money matters in the Abbey. Abbeys like the one in Bury St Edmunds owned lots of land and controlled many villeins. After the Black Death there were fewer villeins to work on the abbey farms. Prior Cambridge insisted that all the surviving villeins should work extra hard to make up for those who had died. Many villeins expected to be treated better now that there were fewer workers. Prior Cambridge disagreed; he said that villeins had no rights and must do as they were told.

Step 2
4 Look at the descriptions of the two people above and highlight or underline reasons why they were attacked by the mob
5 Can you think of anything these people have in common that caused them to be attacked by the peasants?

Medieval People

How hard was life for medieval people?

Step 1

1 From all that you have learnt about medieval life, fill in the chart below with good things and hard things about living in this time.

Life was hard	Life was good
◆	◆
◆	◆
◆	◆
◆	◆
◆	◆

Step 2

2 Choose one of the three storylines below and produce a short story about the life of a peasant in the middle ages.

◆ the story of a peasant who runs away from a village to a town in search of a better life;

◆ the story of someone who lives through and survives the Black Death;

◆ the story of a peasant who gets caught up in the events of the Black Death.

3 Remember to include the key points you have studied throughout this section. In your account include references to the points below:

◆ Life in a medieval town or village.
◆ Chivalry.
◆ Living in London.
◆ Medicine.
◆ The Black Death.
◆ The Peasants' Revolt.